Cisterns
of Gold

Barbara Hinton

PublishAmerica
Baltimore

Softcover 9781462655465
PUBLISHED BY PUBLISHAMERICA, LLLP
www.publishamerica.com
Baltimore

Printed in the United States of America

Cisterns of Gold

John 7:38 Whoever believes in me, as the Scripture has said, streams of living water will flow from within him.

Foreword

"Cisterns of Gold" is a series of stories and songs God has given me from my personal journey of faith. They demonstrate how God used various circumstances and trials in my life to draw me into a more intimate relationship with him and to increase my faith.. It teaches the importance of not just practicing religion, but developing a close personal relationship with Jesus Christ. As we do so, we are able to tap into that unlimited supply of living water that is within each of us as Christians. I hope these stories encourage you in your own Christian walk.

Sincerely,
Barbara Hinton

Chapter 1 Living Cisterns

Thessalonians 4:4 That every one of you should know how to possess his vessel in sanctification and honor.

Cisterns have been used for centuries in many countries for water storage, and many are still being used for that purpose today. The Bible dictionary defines a cistern as a receptacle for water from an external spring or proceeding from rainfall. Fresh water in Judea, Syria, and Palestine was often scarce due to the very dry summer months, so cisterns were very common and necessary for water storage in Biblical times.

I grew up on a ranch, and our water supply was from our own well. The cisterns in the Bible times were often much larger and deeper than the wells we are familiar with today. (http://www.bible-dictionary.org/cistern) Some were so big that there were stairs inside them. The Bible speaks of how some were even large enough to be used as prisons, such as in the story in Genesis 37:22 when Joseph's brothers put him in a cistern to imprison him.

If a cistern was broken, it was of little use. If there were cracked rocks or pieces that were crumbling, then the cistern could only hold a small amount of dirty water, if any at all. If we contain streams of living water within us as John 7:38 teaches, then this means *we are living cisterns. We* are the vessels used to store that living water. *We* are meant to be vessels of honor. God wants us to be holy, to become that unblemished bride of Christ that he has called us to be.

A vessel can be made of many different types of materials. A vessel can be made of clay, of wood, and some are made of precious metals. Personally, I want to be considered a cistern made of gold. Gold is something of great value and is both lovely and durable. A golden vessel is one that is very sturdy, is beautiful, and is suitable for service to royalty. I prefer to think God molded me of clay, then used that clay vessel as a mold for a new vessel of precious gold, one that has been sanctified and has had all of the impurities removed. I want my vessel to be one of honor that is suitable to serve my king, Jesus.

Precious metals in their original state are often full of impurities, and the process used to refine them frequently involves the use of intense heat. God often uses the fire of the trials in our lives to remove our impurities, to refine us, and to draw us closer to him. However, this means that our refining process can often be very uncomfortable and at times even painful. He, the master potter, refines us and molds us into a new creature, that unblemished vessel of honor he has called us to be. The closer we walk to him, the deeper that cistern within us becomes, and the more living water we are capable of holding.

Each follower of Christ has a unique personal journey of faith as he or she develops into that vessel of honor and fulfills God's purpose in their lives. When we accept Christ as our Lord, he accepts us just as we are, regardless of the condition we are in. Our 'vessel' might be tarnished and may even be marred with cracks, chips, and nicks caused by all of our unhealed hurts and by the wrong choices we have made. When we give our lives to Jesus, we place ourselves in the hands of the master potter. It does not make *ANY* difference how damaged our vessel is. He has the ability to reshape us, remold us, and remove all of our blemishes. We become a new creature in him. James 1:2-4 states "*consider it pure joy, my brothers, whenever you face trials of many kinds, because you know that the testing of your faith develops perseverance. Perseverance must finish its work so that you may be mature and complete, not lacking anything. "*

It is important that we allow God to repair our brokenness and to fill all of our nicks, cracks, and chips so our cistern can be filled to the brim. Allow him to shape you into that cistern of gold that contains room for an *unlimited* supply of living water that will not only flow within you, but will then flow out of you to touch others.

Give Me Your Heart

Give me your heart.
I want every part.
I want to be holy.
I want to be holy,
Holy, Lord, like you.
Cleanse me with your fire.
Burn away the mire.
I want to be holy.
I want to be holy,
Holy, Lord, like you.
I will follow hard after you, Lord.
May your will become my own.
How I long to be in your presence,
Kneeling before your throne.
You, Lord, are the potter.
I am just the clay.
Mold me into your image, Lord.
This is what I pray.
Give me your heart.
I want every part.
I want to be holy.
Holy, Lord, like you.

Chapter 2 Broken Cisterns

Jeremiah 2:13 "My people have committed two sins: They have forsaken me, the spring of living water, and have dug their own cisterns, broken cisterns that cannot hold water."

Jeremiah.2:5 tells of how Israel turned away from God to do its own thing.

This is what the LORD says: "What fault did your fathers find in me, that they strayed so far from me? They followed worthless idols and became worthless themselves. 6 They did not ask, 'Where is the LORD, who brought us up out of Egypt and led us through the barren wilderness, through a land of deserts and rifts, a land of drought and darkness, a land where no one travels and no one lives? 7 I brought you into a fertile land to eat its fruit and rich produce. But you came and defiled my land and made my inheritance detestable." They were looking everywhere but to God. They had dug their own cisterns of idolatry and immorality in an attempt to satisfy their desires and needs. However, they found that the cisterns of their own making were broken and couldn't hold even a small amount of refreshing water. Their cisterns were broken from the very moment they were built. This is always the case when we try to build our own cisterns, when we decide to live immoral lives or to allow other things or people to take God's place in our life.

Sometimes I cannot help but wonder what God must think about our nation today. We are very similar to the people described in Jeremiah 2. We were founded as a Christian nation, but in many ways we have allowed God to be taken out of the equation. Our moral values have deteriorated. We have allowed God's values and teachings to be compromised. Many incorrectly think that our Constitution was designed to keep church and state separate. However, the original intent of our forefathers was not to keep the church out of government, but to keep government out of the church so we could worship freely. I personally believe that many of the trials our nation is experiencing today is a result of our building our own cisterns and turning away from God's blessings.

There are times when our cisterns become broken because of our own actions or choices, such as the story in Jeremiah 2. However, there are other times when our cisterns become broken due to circumstances beyond our control and are caused completely by the actions of others. Since broken cisterns cannot hold much water, it is important that we allow God to heal and repair our brokenness, regardless of the cause, so we can become all God has called us to be. We do not want to be limited in the amount of living water our vessel can contain due to the unhealed hurts in our lives. If you tried to pour water into a pitcher that was cracked, you would find out immediately that the use of that pitcher would be very limited. The water within it would leak, and the water would gradually run out. It is the same with us. We too are limited and cannot do all we were designed to do if our vessel has 'leaks'.

When I was 55, I started having flashbacks of abuse I had experienced as a very young child. This was one of the most difficult times in my life. I was in my first term of office as mayor of my city, and although I had shared the flashbacks with a few members of my church family, it was not something I was ready to share publicly. I would put on my 'mask' and go to city hall to fulfill my duties there with a smile on my face. The people I worked with were completely unaware of the inner turmoil and tremendous pain I was experiencing. I was able to let my guard down only when I was in the privacy of my own home. My husband was a tremendous support, even though he didn't fully understand what was going on within me. My prayer closet is the little music studio/office I have set up in my home. Many days I would come home from city hall and go into this room, close the door, and spend hours crying, praying, playing my keyboard, and pouring out my heart to the Lord in worship and prayer. The Bible teaches us that God dwells in the praise of his people. It is in his presence that we are able to tap into the strength and the healing power we need for whatever trial we might be experiencing. As I cried out to the Lord there in my prayer closet, his presence became more real to me than I had ever experienced before.

If a soldier is seriously wounded, he is usually not sent back into the front lines of battle until his wounds have been tended to. I know that's what God did with me. My brokenness, my unhealed hurt from the abuse, had disabled me somewhat as a Christian.

As a leader in my city, I was on the front lines of battle. My wounds needed to heal so I could fulfill the plans and purposes he had for my life. God was 'tending' to my wounds so I would be strong enough to withstand the attacks of the enemy. In this process, as he proved his faithfulness to me and I learned to trust him completely, my cistern grew a little deeper and a little larger. I had been living 'under' the circumstances of my life, instead of allowing God to help me rise 'above' the circumstances as an overcomer through his grace and mercy.

Music has always played a special part in my life, and it also played an important part in my healing journey. A minister I knew who was also an overcomer of childhood abuse encouraged me to write out my pain. Many people find journaling therapeutic. Writing songs had that same therapeutic effect on me that journaling has on others. I would sit at my keyboard and worship, pouring out all of my pain through songs. The music just poured out of me during that period in my life. I have written many songs over the years, but the ones that are the most meaningful to me personally are those written when God was leading me through that deep valley to healing. Those few months when I dealt with all of the agony and emotions connected with the flashbacks made me recognize that I was not where I should be spiritually. Even though I had been a Christian most of my life, I had just been practicing religion. God used that period in my life to teach me the difference between going through the motions of religion and actually developing a personal, intimate relationship with my Savior. I really thought I had always trusted God. However, I see now that for years I had given this situation (my childhood hurts) to God, only to yank it back again and attempt to deal with my problems in my own strength. My abuser had passed away years before, and I went through a period of denial after his death. I was aware he had other victims, but I tried to convince myself that maybe I was mistaken and nothing had really happened to me. The flashbacks made me realize that I had not been mistaken. I was finally able to say "Lord, I can't carry this any longer. You take it." It was at this point when the inner pain was so unbearable that I was finally willing to trust God completely, without any reservations or conditions. He was then able to complete the healing he had started within me. I once heard a minister preach that the process God often uses to change us is a three step one — *reveal, deal,* and *heal.* This proved to be very true in my case. The flashbacks *revealed* to me I had a problem. I then had to go through a period of time when I had to personally *deal* with the hurt that accompanied the memories. I first had to recognize that I had a problem that could no longer be overlooked, and one that I alone could not fix. When I accepted this fact and finally gave my burden to God instead of trying to personally 'control' everything myself, God was able to complete the inner healing I so desperately needed. Several months after wrestling with the emotions that flooded my mind as a result of the flashbacks, I was ready to turn all of my hurt over to God and ask him to heal me. I went forward one Sunday morning and asked one of our elders to anoint me with oil and pray over me as the scriptures instruct for healing. The oil that was used was unscented, but I immediately smelled a fragrance surround me as the elder put the anointing oil on my forehead and prayed over me. I went shopping several hours after church was over, and I could still smell that fragrance encircling me. I felt like I was actually walking inside a hula hoop of fragrance. It was a supernatural experience I had never experienced before, but one that I have encountered two other times since in my life. On that day God completed the healing he had started in me several months earlier.

I'm still amazed as I look back at how God used music as such an important part of my healing process. My abuser was actually the individual who had taught me as a child to have a deep love for Christian music. He was the person who gave me my first piano, making me promise that I would learn to play it well enough to play at church. He was a song leader at his church. I don't refer to him as a worship leader, because his love for music was more about performing and the recognition he received than a means of bringing glory to God. His love for music had become a type of idolatry. Singing and performing were his 'gods', instead of his singing being a sincere act of worship to the Lord. It was fitting that God took that one thing that was so important to the person responsible for my emotional hurts and used it as an instrument of healing for me. The following lyrics are the words to a song I wrote out of the hurt I was experiencing, singing it over and over as I dealt with the memories. It is one that played an important part in my healing process.

Your Grace Is Sufficient

At times when I grow weary and start to feel despair
Haunting memories of the past renew old pain.
Then I lift my eyes towards heaven,
And you heal my broken spirit.
There is nothing, Lord, with you I cannot share.
Your grace is sufficient, your grace is sufficient,
Your grace is sufficient, Lord, for me.
Your grace is sufficient, your grace is sufficient.
Your matchless grace reached down and rescued me.

There were days when I wondered how I could still go on.
The hurt was more than I alone could bear,
But you promised you'd go with me
And lead me through the valleys.
I heard you say, "My child, you know I care."
Your love is sufficient, your love is sufficient,
Your love is sufficient, Lord, for me.
Your love is sufficient, your love is sufficient.
Your unending love reached down and lifted me.

Chapter 3 God Is At Work Behind the Scenes

Romans 8:28 And we know that in all things God works for the good of those who love Him, who have been called according to His purpose.

Romans 8:28 was the first scripture I memorized after being baptized at age 21, and it has continued to be one of my personal 'life' scriptures. I once read that our lives are like a fine tapestry made of all of our experiences. This has proven to be very true in my own life. I remember events that I considered very painful at the time they occurred. However, in looking back I can now see they were sometimes blessings in disguise. God was working for my good in these situations. I just could not recognize the blessing in the midst of my pain and disappointments.

I recall being promised a long waited for promotion. At that time the company I worked for had an affirmative action policy in place and had specific targets to meet to make sure there was a balance of minorities in management. When the management opening occurred, my employer had some affirmative action quotas that had not been met, and as a result the job my boss had planned to give to me had to be given to someone from another town in order to meet those corporate quotas. Saying I was disappointed is a big understatement. However, I can look back on that situation now and see how God's hand of protection operated on my behalf. What occurred was actually a blessing in disguise. The corporation I worked for ended up splitting into several companies, and the position I had wanted was eventually phased out and the person who had been promoted was eventually transferred out of town. I would have been required to transfer to another location, which was not a possibility for me because of my husband's employment. If I had received the promotion at that time, I could easily have been left without a job, losing many future retirement benefits. I was later promoted in God's perfect timing to a management position that fit not only my work experience, but my family needs as far as location and work hours. I held that position until retirement.

Several years before I retired, my husband invited me to attend a county board of supervisors meeting with him. His attendance at the meeting was a job responsibility for him, but he thought the meeting would be of personal interest to me since my cousin had just been elected to the board of supervisors. That meeting changed my life and direction. Seeing my cousin, someone who had spent a lot of time in my home one summer when I was growing up, made me realize that anyone can be in public service if they are interested and willing to serve. It is not something reserved just for 'certain people'. Needless to say, I was 'bit' by the bug of politics and public service that evening. Shortly after that meeting my local newspaper advertised an opening on the planning commission, and I applied. I remember our mayor, whom I had never met, came to my home to interview me. I received the appointment and spent the next 6 ½ years as a planning commissioner, including acting as the chairperson of the commission for much of that time. I started feeling a desire to run for the city council, but learned that I could not do so without corporate approval from my employer and this approval was denied. When I was 48, I heard rumors that my employer was planning to offer early retirement to managers. I was interested in the early retirement package, and once again the Lord started putting the desire in my heart to run for a city council seat. One of my good friends at work, a strong Christian and intercessor, had prayed with me regarding this. We both felt the Lord was leading me to a position on the city council. It was an election year, so I attempted to confirm the early retirement offer in the hopes of being able to file campaign papers, accept early retirement, and run for office. Unfortunately, the company would not confirm the rumor of the early retirement package, so I was not able to file candidate's papers before the filing deadline. A few weeks before the actual election, the company finally officially announced the early retirement offer and one of the requirements was that we be off the payroll by Dec. 31 if we wished to participate. I applied for the retirement package, and in Nov. one of the city council members was elected mayor. This created a vacancy on the city council that was to be filled by appointment. I applied for the position, and was appointed to the city council to finish out the term of the newly elected mayor. I served a total of six years as a councilwoman & vice mayor. When our mayor announced he was not seeking re-election, I was encouraged by many friends and leaders in the community to run for the position. I wanted to be sure that this was what God wanted me to do, and I asked my pastor to pray with me for clear direction from the Lord. My pastor too felt I was being called to run for mayor, and as he began to pray he asked God to open the doors no one could shut and to close the doors no man could open if I was to seek this office. He also prayed that I would receive a confirmation if I was in fact to run for this office as we both thought. I was being called to do. Later that same day I called my friend, Charlene, the former co-worker who had helped pray me into office so many years before when I first sought a council seat. I told her I was seeking direction from the Lord regarding the upcoming election for a new mayor in my city. I did not tell her what my pastor had said, but asked her to pray as I wanted clear direction from the Lord. She said her husband had been given a scripture when he was facing a similar decision at work, and thought that same scripture would be helpful to me as well. She left the phone for a few moments to locate the scripture. When she returned, she told me she had been unable to find the scripture, but she had found a piece of paper lying next to the phone. She picked up the paper, and on it was written the scripture she had been seeking. The scripture on that piece of paper was Revelation 3:7-8 *"What he opens no one can shut, and what he shuts no one can open. I know your deeds. See, I have placed before you an open door that no one can shut."* I then shared with my friend what my pastor had said when he prayed with me, and we both felt the scripture on the paper confirmed that I was to run for the office of mayor. I was successful in being elected to two terms as nayor, the first woman in my city's history to hold this office. Just before I left public office at the end of my second term as mayor, a local hospital chaplain invited me to be the keynote speaker at an annual prayer breakfast he was hosting at the hospital. I prayed about what I was to speak on, and I believed the Holy Spirit spoke very clearly to my heart that it was time for me to share the testimony of the abuse, my flashbacks, and my healing in a public setting. I thought I would just be addressing hospital personnel, but when I arrived at that conference location I discovered I would be speaking to a fairly large community group. I recognized many community leaders, including a well-known former mayor from the large city that neighbors mine. As they entered that room I began to feel very uneasy as I realized just who I would be addressing, and I really wasn't sure I could go through with it. I had received a prophetic word a couple of days before the breakfast as a minister friend prayed with me. I was told that God was going to use me at that breakfast, and as I was obedient to the Holy Spirit all I would have to do would be to open my mouth to speak and God would fill it. That's exactly what happened. I didn't understand why I was to share my story at that particular time. However, God did, and I was obedient to the prompting of the Holy Spirit. I have given many public presentations over the years, but I have never felt a stronger anointing than I did as I spoke at that prayer breakfast that morning. I shared in detail the importance that prayer and worship had played in my healing, and I also read the words to "Your Grace Is Sufficient". At a couple of points I could feel my eyes filling with tears as I spoke. As I looked at the audience, I could see several others responding in the same way with tears of their own. I can't tell you how many people, both men and women, came up to me later and privately shared that they too were dealing with issues of abuse in their own lives. I remember one young man in particular who spoke to me. He was very careful that no one would overhear him, and he said he was really struggling with abuse issues from his own childhood. He said hearing my testimony had encouraged him to seek some counseling. I had others who asked if they could have copies of my song. As I offered individual words of encouragement to those who spoke to me, I understood why the Lord had asked me to share my testimony. He was in total control. He knew who had been given divine appointments to be at that prayer breakfast, and he knew just what those whom he had called needed to hear in order to meet them at their own place of need. He had appointed me to be his instrument of encouragement that morning. He had given me the assignment that day to be that living cistern of gold, allowing those streams of living waters that were flowing within me to pour out to those in the audience who were hurting and in need of God's healing touch.

Send Your Anointing

Lord, send your anointing.
Let it fall on me.
Anointing, fall on me.
Spirit of the living God,
Rise up in me.
Lord, send your anointing.
Let it fall on me.

May it pour down like a river
Until it floods my soul.
May streams of living water
Fill this cistern of gold.
Let it pour out through me
To set captives free.
Lord, send your anointing.
Let it fall on me.

Lord, send your anointing.
Let it fall on me.
Anointing, fall on me.
Spirit of the Living God,
Rise up in me.
Lord, send your anointing,
Let it fall on me.
Anointing, fall on me.
May streams of healing water

Fill this cistern of gold
Use me to touch the sick,
Lord, and make them whole.
Let it pour out through me
To set others free.
Send your anointing,
Let it fall on me.

Empty Vessels of Clay

We're empty vessels of clay.
Lord, please fill us today
With hidden treasures
From your kingdom foretold.
You're the potter, we're the clay.
Lord, please fill us we pray
With things more precious than silver or gold.
Vessels of honor used in service to our King.
Lord, our desire is glory to you bring.
We're empty vessels of clay.
Lord, please fill us today
With hidden treasures
From your kingdom foretold.
You're the potter. We're the clay.
Lord, please fill us we pray
With things more precious than silver or gold.
Give us your compassion for the woman at the well.
Fill us with your boldness as the gospel we tell.
May we be your hand of healing so blind eyes may see.
Let us be your love extended, setting captives free.
We're empty vessels of clay.
Lord, please use us today.
Give us hidden treasures untold.
You're the potter, we're the clay.
Lord, please fill us today
With things more precious than silver or gold.

Chapter 4 God Never Allows a Hurt to Be Wasted

2 Corinthians 1:3-4 Praise be to the Father of our Lord Jesus Christ, the Father of compassion and the God of all comfort, who comforts us in all our troubles, so that we can comfort those in any trouble with the comfort we ourselves have received from God.

I am amazed at the number of abuse victims, both male and female, whom I have had the opportunity to minister to since I first experienced the flashbacks, and since I first shared my testimony publicly at the prayer breakfast. God has taken my healed hurt and allowed me to reach out and minister to others who were going through similar trials. He doesn't allow our hurts to be wasted. I have a much greater understanding and empathy for those struggling with abuse issues than I ever could have had if it were not for my own similar hurts.

I was co-director of the women's ministry at my church for several years. I am also very involved in Aglow International, an interdenominational Christian organization. Through my work with these two ministries I have had an opportunity to minister to many women and to some men who had issues of abuse they are trying to overcome. My former pastor also asked me to facilitate a Bible study at our church that I named Potter's House. It was specifically for women who were struggling with abuse issues. I facilitated several three month classes, leading women through a study of scriptures about trust, forgiveness, shame, control, anger, guilt, etc. Each of these subjects is a major issue so common to those overcoming issues of abuse. Some of the abuse experienced by these women was physical, some sexual, and some verbal or emotional. Regardless of the type of abuse experienced or the actual degree of the abuse, I found the issues they struggled with were often very similar and there were wounds that were left that need to be tended to and healed. I personally was never angry with God for what happened to me as a little girl, but this is not the case with many abuse victims. Anger towards God is a big area that often needs to be addressed before healing can really take place. It is also difficult for many abuse victims to accept God's unconditional love. They mistakenly conclude that he couldn't possibly love them or he would not have allowed them to be abused. They sometimes have deep anger issues towards God for what they experienced. They also often believe that the abuse they suffered was their fault. These are all lies from Satan. The Bible tells us that God will NEVER leave us or forsake us. I know that God did not want me to be abused. He hates all sin, and what my abuser did to me was sin. I believe God grieved deeply for what happened to me. I know he didn't leave me, and I know he did not forsake me. I also know that what happened to me was the result of another person's free will and that person's conscious decision to commit a sinful act.

Forgiveness is an extremely difficult issue for victims of abuse, and one I have really personally struggled with in many different areas of my life. However, forgiveness is not really an option for the believer. If we want God to forgive us when we sin, we must forgive those who hurt us. Matthew 6:14 – 15 puts it pretty bluntly. *For if you forgive men when they sin against you, your heavenly Father will also forgive you. But if you do not forgive men their sins, your Father will not forgive your sins.* By forgiving, you are not saying that what happened to you is okay. It also does not mean you are required to continue a personal friendship or relationship with that person. Trust was destroyed with that individual and must be restored for a relationship to take place. What it does mean is that you release any feeling of debt you feel that person may owe you, and you put things in God's hands. Each of us is held accountable to God for our own actions only, not for the actions of others. I have learned in my own journey of faith that sometimes when the hurt is very deep, we do not have the ability to accomplish forgiveness in our own strength. My abuser was a family member, and my parents also suffered a lot of hurt as they blamed themselves for what happened. My abuser was someone my parents loved and should have been able to trust. Again, no one else was at fault except my abuser. I believe the Lord has taught me that forgiveness is often simply a matter of choice. I told God that I could not achieve forgiveness for my abuser in my own strength. The hurt was very deep. I had not been his only victim. This was someone I loved very much, and the reality of all he had done to me and to other family members was very painful as well as impossible for me to understand. However, I also told God that I *chose* to forgive the person who had abused me. I asked him to complete that forgiveness and healing work within me. It was not something that was accomplished over night. It was a process, and God was faithful to complete that forgiveness in me.

Create A New Thing In Me

Isaiah 43: 18 *"Forget the former things; do not dwell on the past. 19 See, I am doing a new thing! Now it springs up; do you not perceive it? I am making a way in the desert and streams in the wasteland*

Create a new thing in me, O Lord.
Create a new thing in me.
I'll remember not the former things,
For they have passed away.
I'll dwell not on the things of old,
The hurts of yesterday.
Create a new thing in me, O God.
Create a new thing in me.
Make me all that you want me to be.
Set my Spirit free.
Make me all that you want me to be.
Create a new thing in me.

Chapter 5 God's Masterpieces

Isaiah 64:8 Yet, O Lord, you are our Father.
*We are the **clay**, you are the potter; we are all*
the work of your hand.

When I was a teenager, I remember my grandmother making what was called 'crazy quilts' to give to her grandchildren. These were to be used as bedspreads, but were also something that could be saved to hand down as family heirlooms. She ordered huge boxes of fabric scraps, and you would never know what colors would be in the boxes she received. I remember one box was filled with pieces of taffeta of varying colors. The quilt I received had strips of red, pale pink, light lime green, white, and pale blue taffeta. There really wasn't a pattern to the way the strips were sewn together, and that was why they were called 'crazy' quilts. However, at the time she made them, I thought they were crazy because of the color combinations she would use. Her goal was to take whatever she received in the fabric boxes, regardless of the colors of fabric received, and form them into something that was useful, unique, and would serve to remind us of her in years to come. She was careful not to waste even the smallest piece of fabric. Somehow, she always cut the irregular sized pieces so they fit together perfectly to form her quilt. She sewed them together skillfully and then took them to a seamstress to add the finishing touches to them and to put on a backing to her quilt. The finished products were very unique and well made.

Years after my grandmother's death, I attended a community fund raising event at a local park. There were many booths and displays set up. As I walked into the park, I suddenly stopped in my tracks. I found myself being somewhat overwhelmed by emotion, and my eyes started to fill with tears as I gazed at the sight before me. To my surprise, there was a group of 'crazy quilts' on display in the booth in front of me. I knew immediately, without any doubt whatsoever in my mind, that these were some of my deceased grandmother's creations. They were easily recognizable to me because of the 'unique' color combinations she always used. I examined them carefully and found her name pinned to some of the quilts. I inquired about where the quilts had come from, and found that one of the hostesses in the booth was the seamstress who had always finished my grandmother's quilts. She had borrowed some from one of my aunts to use in the historical display.

The way my grandmother constructed her crazy quilts is very similar to what God does in our lives when we accept Jesus as our Lord and Savior. Our pieces are often irregular and don't always seem to match. We often come to him with a lot of brokenness caused by our sins, our hurts, and our past hardships. As I explained earlier, our brokenness is sometimes caused by the actions of others and through no fault of our own, and sometimes it is a direct result of choices we have made. We are so fortunate that God accepts us just the way we are, and by his grace takes our 'irregular' shaped broken pieces and molds them into something new, a beautiful vessel that can be used to serve him. Just as my grandmother was careful not to waste the smallest piece of material, God doesn't waste any of our hurts. You would wonder how our broken pieces could ever 'go together', but in God's hands our brokenness is molded and used to create something new that is both useful and unique. We become his masterpiece, just like my grandmother's quilts were her masterpiece. His finished product will also easily be recognized by others, just as I recognized my grandmother's handiwork, because it will reflect his character and workmanship.

Broken Pieces

Lord, I give to you all the broken
pieces of my life.
I lay them all down, Jesus, at your feet-
My shattered dreams, my hurt, my guilt, my shame
O take them all, Lord, and make me whole again.
You are the potter.
They're just tiny, broken bits of clay.
So please take them all Lord,
And make me whole today.
Take these broken pieces and mold them
Create something new
Something beautiful
Designed to be used by you.
I want to be that vessel of honor, Lord,
Used in service to my King.
I just want to serve you, Lord,

And glory to you bring.
So take my broken pieces.
I humbly give them all to you.
I know in your hands
You'll take all of my pain
You'll mend my broken pieces,
And make me whole again.

Chapter 6 Training Ground

1 Peter 2:5 You yourselves like living stones are being built up as a spiritual house, to be a holy priesthood, to offer spiritual sacrifices acceptable to God through Jesus Christ.

About sixteen years ago a friend invited me to attend a meeting of the local chapter of Aglow International. Aglow was having a special speaker my friend wanted to hear, and she did not want to attend the meeting alone. That was the beginning for me of an association with Aglow that I still enjoy today.

At the second Aglow International meeting I attended, I went to the altar following the meeting and requested prayer for my daughter and son-in-law's marriage. The speaker told me I had been carrying the burden for my daughter for too long, and I needed to give the situation to God. I recall the speaker praying with me after the meeting and telling me that God was going to raise me up to be an intercessor for my family. I really didn't understand fully what she meant. So, she was telling me I was going to pray for my family? I thought to myself, "I already do that. We all pray." However, I learned that becoming an intercessor meant taking my prayer life to an entirely different level. It meant that I wouldn't just spend a few minutes adding that prayer need to my regular prayers every day, but it could mean sometimes spending hours petitioning the Lord on behalf of someone else. It could mean weeping before the Lord as I prayed and worshipped. It meant that sometimes I would wake up in the middle of the night, suddenly feeling the strong need to pray and intercede for a particular person. Interceding for our families is a good starting place for intercession because we are usually emotionally involved enough with our loved ones that we will be disciplined to be diligent about our prayer.

If we are faithful about a little, he will often give us more. That's what he did with me as an intercessor. Interceding for my family was my training ground, and as I persevered and prayed for them God expanded my prayer targets as an intercessor. I had spent over twelve years in local government as an appointed and elected official before being elected mayor of my community. I knew God had allowed me to be elected for a purpose, but I just didn't know then what the purpose was. I considered my time in office as a ministry, no different than any other ministry assignment I had ever accepted at church. Since I had been a council member and vice mayor, I was completely prepared for the 'mechanics' of the office of nayor. However, even with my experience I was still very surprised by some of the 'dynamics' that went along with the new position. There were often complex issues as I frequently dealt with those who had personal agendas to promote. There were also situations where there were safety issues, and I had to proceed with caution. I recall two occasions when a police report was filed on my behalf because of incidents that could be perceived as potential threats to my safety. I was also the first woman in my city's history to be elected mayor, and I had additional challenges. I dealt with some who had difficulty accepting a woman at the helm of our city's government, and some who attempted to 'strongly influence' my decisions. At that time the term of office was just two years, so the moment one election ended individuals who had political aspirations were already trying to position themselves for the next election.

Most of our council meetings were peaceful, but I recall a few meetings when extremely controversial issues were being considered and we had to take additional security precautions. I remember one meeting when we were expecting a particular citizen to address the council. He had already attempted to physically assault a city employee and had called city hall the day of the meeting and made threats regarding our meeting. As a precaution, our city manager had arranged for police officers to be present. I recall going into the empty council chambers early in the day when no one was around and quietly anointing the entrances with anointing oil and praying over the entire room. I had a real burden for the meeting that was scheduled, and I privately went into deep intercession in that empty meeting room. The citizen did not show up after all, and the meeting was very peaceful. There was no doubt in my mind that this was an answer to prayer. There were many times when I would either close my office door at city hall to intercede quietly for our community or would pray privately in the council chambers prior to a meeting when conflict was anticipated. One of my vice mayors, who was a strong Christian and former youth pastor, and I were nicknamed 'The God Squad' by some in the community who opposed us. The name, a takeoff from the old T.V. series by a similar name, was meant to be an insult, but we took it as a compliment. When I had to appoint someone to a commission or key position, I often went into my prayer closet without anyone's knowledge and privately prayed about each applicant I was considering. There were a couple of times when I went into prayer thinking I knew which applicant to choose, and after my prayer time made an entirely different decision.

The Army of Love

The army of love are we_____
Going to battle on our knees.
Fighting the good fight day after day.
We're the army of love that prays.
Praying and fasting,
Heeding God's call.
Trusting, obeying,
Giving our all.
The army of love are we.
The army of love are we___
Praying our Father's will be done
Right here on earth as it is in heaven.
Having faith that our prayers
Will bring victory.
The army of love are we.
The army of love are we _____
Going to battle on our knees.
Fighting the good fight day after day.
We're the army of love that prays.
We're the army of love that prays,
The army of love that prays.

Chapter 7 God Works in Miraculous Ways

Psalms 103:2-5 "Bless the Lord oh my soul
and forget not all His benefits, who forgives all
your sins, who heals all your diseases."

While I was in office, my husband went to the doctor for a routine exam. One of the test results was not good, and he was referred to a specialist for a colonoscopy. When this test was completed, the specialist called me into his office to review my husband's results. He showed me pictures of a large mass that totally engulfed one section of my husband's colon. The specialist said it was extremely large, had been there for a very long time, and was more than likely malignant. A date was set to have the mass surgically removed. Before the scheduled surgery date, we had a guest speaker at our church. Her name was Rev. Neva Lema, and my associate pastor asked her to pray with me after the service, explaining to her that my husband was facing surgery. I had never met her before that day. As she prayed for me, she started prophesying over the situation telling me I was not to pay any attention to what the situation looked like or sounded like, that God was taking care of it and was using this to build my husband's faith. After she prayed with me, I had such an assurance that Jack was going to be healed, that when the family was sitting in the hospital waiting room during his surgery I told them not to be surprised if the doctor told us he could not find a mass. I was that confident that we were going to witness a miracle. I ran across our family physician in the hall at the hospital and learned he had assisted in Jack's surgery. He told me I was lucky that they had found the tumor when they did. He said it had just started to grow and was not even as large as my little finger nail. He said it was malignant, and if they had not found it when they did I would have been a widow within a couple of years. He said they were able to remove it completely. I was elated! *I knew that I knew* that my God had shrunk the mass! I still had the film from the colonoscopy showing that the affected portion of the colon was completely engulfed with the tumor, and the specialist had told me it was *very large and had been there for a long time.* My faith soared.

That cistern within me grew deeper. My husband had always been a believer and was a real student of the Bible, but he had never really stepped into the role of spiritual head of our household. He had been raised in a very conservative church that did not teach about the spiritual gifts, especially those of healing and prophecy. When Neva Lema prayed with me about my husband's colon surgery, she also told me that God was going to use his illness to increase his faith.

Awesome God

Lord, you are an awesome God,
And I stand in awe of you.
Lord, you are an awesome God,
Faithful and true.
You never change,
You're always the same.
I can count on you.
Lord, you are an awesome God,
And I stand in awe of you.
I look around in wonder
As I see your mighty hand
Moving to move my mountains
According to your perfect plan.
Lord, you are an awesome God,
And I stand in awe of you.
Lord you are an awesome God
Faithful and true.
Lord you are and awesome God
And I stand in awe of you.
So I'll take up my cross
And daily follow you.

Chapter 8 Be Careful What You Pray. Your Answer May Not Be What You Expect.

1 Peter 2:5 You yourselves like living stones are being built up as a spiritual house, to be a holy priesthood, to offer spiritual sacrifices acceptable to God through Jesus Christ.

During my second term as mayor, our associate pastor prophesied over me that God was going to lighten my load and shorten my day. He said the Lord said I had turned my position as mayor into a much more labor intensive job than God had intended it to be for me. I had always been somewhat of a workaholic. I was the only member of the council who did not work, so I accepted many of the committee assignments that required meeting during normal business hours. At one time I was serving on thirteen committees and boards in addition to my other mayoral duties. I was also division president for the League of California Cities. My involvement really impacted my family time. I felt guilty when I had to leave one of my granddaughter's softball games before it ended because I had a meeting to attend.

I started praying, seeking God's will about running for a third term as mayor. I had already spent sixteen years in public service, including the years I served on our planning commission. I was very tired and ready to step down, but only if I felt the Lord was releasing me. I still considered my time in office as a ministry, and like any other ministry I was involved in, I would not step down unless I felt God was releasing me from that assignment. I had hoped he would release me prior to the deadline for filing candidate's papers so I could just quietly retire. I was very thankful that my husband had been healed of the colon cancer. He was retired, and I wanted to be able to spend some quality time with him and our family. However, I didn't sense God releasing me from my position, so I moved forward, filed candidate's papers for the upcoming election, and ran an active campaign for a third term. Two days before the election, Rev. Neva Lema, the minister who had ministered to me when Jack was facing colon surgery and on another occasion as well, was the guest speaker at a local church. I attended that service, and she called me out of the audience, asking me why God continued to put her in my path every time I was thinking about retiring. She said God was not through with me yet, that he still needed me to stand up for righteousness. Those present at that meeting, including myself, thought that she was telling me I was going to be elected again. *1Corinthians. 13:9*

"For we know in part and we prophecy in part." The prophetic word Neva Lema spoke to me was an example of prophesying in part. She said God still needed me to stand up for righteousness, but she did ***not*** prophesy how this would happen. ***We*** assumed that the prophetic word meant I would be re-elected, but I was not. On election night as the precinct results were posted and I was behind, I didn't believe the reports. In fact, some of my friends who were in the audience when Neva Lema spoke were at my home on election night, and they started singing the song "Whose report will you believe? I will believe the report of the Lord." I would not concede the election until days later when all of the absentee ballots were counted. I was still convinced I was going to win the election based on ***my*** understanding of the prophetic word I had been given. However, I lost, and I was devastated. I wasn't devastated because I was leaving office or because

I had lost the election. Remember, I had truly hoped to be released. I just didn't want it to happen this way. It was the first time in my life that my faith and my core beliefs were shaken to the roots. A few days later I broke out with shingles, and I know this condition was brought about by the stress of the campaign and election. Talk about feeling rejected! I felt that this city of 35,000 that I loved dearly and had been devoted to for so many years had rejected me. I had sincerely hoped God would tell me not to run, let me retire, and go on with my life. It definitely had not been my desire to run for office and lose. However, God's ways are not our ways. I went into a deep depression for a couple of months, not so much because of the outcome of the election, but because I began to question my religious beliefs. I truly thought the prophetic word I had received from this very reliable source, someone who had ministered to me several times and I highly respected, had not come to pass. It made me start to question my core beliefs. It was the first time in my life that my faith was tested to the bootstraps, and looking back I can see that this was necessary. God had to be sure I was completely grounded and secure in my faith and beliefs, and this trial only served to strengthen me for where he was about to send me. I literally wrestled with my own emotions and beliefs, but when I was through battling with myself I continued to believe in all of the spiritual gifts described in 1 Cor.12, including the gift of prophecy. However, the Bible also teaches that we know or understand in part and prophecy in part. I later realized that this prophecy was in part, and I had understood it in part. It did not say I was going to win, and it did not say how I was to stand for righteousness. God was about to provide an opportunity for me to continue to stand up for righteousness at a higher level of government.

Thank You For Your Faithfulness
Lord, thank you for your faithfulness,
Your faithfulness to me.
When I see where I have been
And know where that I might be
If it wasn't for your love that reached down and lifted me.
I humbly bow before your now,
And thank you for your faithfulness to me.
That path I had followed was a road of no return.
The hurt that I felt there was more than I had ever known.
Then I looked into your face, saw your amazing grace.
You wiped away my tears and took away my fears
Now I just have to say_____
Lord, thank your for your faithfulness, your faithfulness to
me.
When I see where I have been
And know where that I might be
If it wasn't for your love that reached down and lifted me.
I humbly bow before you now,
And thank you for your faithfulness to me.

Chapter 9 Moving Up to Higher Ground

1 Timothy 2:1-3
1 I urge, then, first of all, that petitions, prayers, intercession and thanksgiving be made for all people— 2 for kings and all those in authority, that we may live peaceful and quiet lives in all godliness and holiness. 3 This is good, and pleases God our Savior.

I know that the time I spent in local government was merely training ground for where the Lord had planned to send me. The next place I was going was to Sacramento, the capital city of California, to stand for righteousness in our state. However, I was going there not as an elected official, but as an intercessor for our state government.. Immediately after leaving office, I was asked to accept a leadership position with the local chapter of Aglow International. My involvement with Aglow led to a new opportunity to serve as an intercessor. I was asked to help establish a prayer ministry for Aglow inside the California Capitol building. Five of us visited there, praying very quietly around the building and grounds and inquiring about what was needed to be granted permission to meet and pray regularly inside the Capitol. I learned by visiting one of the offices there that we would have to secure sponsorship from a legislator to be allowed to meet inside the Capitol. I knew a couple of legislators personally, and I am sure either would have agreed to sponsor us if I had asked. However, as I prayed, I felt strongly that I was not to approach either of the men I knew well. We were able to obtain sponsorship from a Christian assemblyman who lived in the large city next to mine. I had met him once or twice and we knew each other by reputation, but I did not actually know him personally. By our third trip to Sacramento, we had permission to meet monthly for prayer in one of the Assembly conference rooms. A small group of dedicated Aglow intercessors faithfully traveled from various cities each month to pray for our government. My seventeen years in local government gave me insight on how to pray for our elected officials, their staff, and their families.

Our state capital is located approximately eighty miles from my home, and my prayer partner Kim Staats drove me there each month for our intercessors' meeting. On one of our very first trips, God demonstrated to us in a very real way that he was with us in this ministry, and his hand of protection was upon us. As Kim and I traveled on Highway 99 to Sacramento, three different trucks started drifting across the white line into our lane, almost sideswiping our car on the passenger's side where I was sitting. When the third truck started veering into our lane, I extended my hand towards it and Kim and I started praying in the spirit. It was clear to us that this was not a coincidental thing, but a spiritual battle. The Bible tells us that we do not battle flesh and blood, but principalities and powers of darkness. As we prayed, the truck immediately pulled back into its' own lane. At that same moment, I smelled a beautiful fragrance fill our car. It was the same experience I had previously when God completed the healing of my emotional hurts following the flashbacks. Kim also smelled the fragrance, and we were able to identify it as the Rose of Sharon. Kim had a bottle of anointing oil of the same fragrance, so it was a fragrance we both recognized.

On the return trip that same day, we had another supernatural experience. Oleanders form the median on Highway 99, and they had burst into flames in front of us.

We could hear fire trucks in the distance, and smoke was all the way across our lane of traffic. There was no way that Kim could stop or safely pull off the road, so we had to continue driving towards the flames and smoke. Again, we stretched out our hands and prayed in the spirit. The smoke and flames totally opened up, providing a clear path for our car. I turned around as we passed the flaming oleanders, and the lane behind us was again totally engulfed in smoke. Again, the car filled with the fragrance of the Rose of Sharon. God was demonstrating in a very real way that we had spiritual authority, and he was there with us through whatever we encountered. Again, that cistern within me grew larger and my faith once again was strengthened. The Lord had impressed upon me when we first started the Aglow Capitol ministry that I was to establish it, and I would only be there personally for three or four years. That is exactly what occurred. I led Aglow's Capitol ministry for four years. However, it has now been eleven years since it was established, and it is still going strong. I continue, as Aglow's government coordinator for California, to assist with preparing the prayer agenda each month for the Capitol Aglow Lighthouse, but I no longer travel to Sacramento for the monthly meetings.

Leading Aglow's Capitol prayer ministry was one of the most rewarding ministry assignments I have ever had. As a non-profit organization, Aglow does not support or oppose any individual candidate, but we pray for all those in authority as the scriptures instruct us to do. One interesting experience I had during that time was having the privilege of helping to host a prayer shield for Arnold. Schwarzenegger during his first inauguration ceremony as governor. I was approached by a couple of Sacramento area ministers who invited our Capitol Aglow Lighthouse to participate in the prayer shield they were organizing. They said they were trying to find a legislator to act as sponsor so a place inside the Capitol building could be made available. I offered to have our Aglow

Lighthouse officially host the event for them, since we already had a sponsor and were regularly assigned a conference room. Our sponsor's office was contacted and we were provided a different conference room on inauguration day, one that was large enough to accommodate the group we were anticipating. It was located near the top of the building. I had the privilege of serving as the facilitator and worship leader at the event, and God gave me a new song to use as a theme song for the prayer shield meeting. The pastors invited intercessors from several Sacramento area ministries and churches to participate. Of course, when you are swearing in a well known celebrity as governor, you are going to attract other celebrities and crowds to the event. The area around the capitol was filled with lines of people trying to gain admittance to the ceremonies, and security was increased. We could not see any of the inaugural activities from our conference room, and we were there in prayer for about three hours. Immediately following the event, a group of my Aglow friends and I started walking back to our hotel to pick up our cars. We were on a short back street that was not traveled much. We were just starting to walk across the street when a policeman on a motorcycle came around the corner and instructed us to get back onto the sidewalk. All of a sudden a chauffeur driven vehicle came around the corner, and we were surprised to see that the passengers were the governor and his wife. Needless to say, our group was very excited. We had not been able to see anything from our conference room, but God allowed us to be close enough to wave at the governor and he waved back and called out to us. It was the perfect ending to a wonderful day.

America
(Written for the Prayer Shield in Sacramento)

America, America -
Land of the brave and the free
America, my America
I'm calling you back to me.
If my people who are called by my name
Will just humble
Themselves and pray
If they'll humble themselves and pray
And turn from their wicked ways.
If they'll humble themselves and pray
And turn from their wicked ways,
Then will I hear and heal their land.

America, our America-
Land of the brave and the free.
America, our America -
It's time to get down on our knees.

Lord, we humble ourselves and pray,
And we turn from our wicked ways.
We humble ourselves and pray,
And we turn from our wicked ways.
We humble ourselves and pray,
And we turn from our wicked ways.
Come Lord, O come and heal our land.

America, our America
Land of the brave and the free
America, our America
Our answers will be found on our knees.
Yes, our answers will be found on our knees.

Chapter 10 Illness Strikes Again

Psalms 41:3
The LORD will strengthen him on his bed
of illness; You will sustain him on his sickbed.

The healing of colon cancer I described previously was just the first example in a series of healings in my husband's life. A few years later, he started having chest pains and I took him to the emergency room. He wouldn't let me call an ambulance, so I drove him to the hospital. After sitting for a few minutes in the waiting room, he said the pain had stopped, that he had probably just had a caffeine reaction, and we might as well go home. At that very moment, the triage nurse called his name. I told him since we were at the hospital, that we should still let them check him out as a precaution. They did some blood tests, and we understood he was about to be released. He put on his shoes and was sitting on the side of the hospital bed waiting to receive his release papers when he suddenly had a full blown heart attack. While hospital staff worked on him, I immediately ran out into the hall and made a couple of phone calls to ask my church and my Aglow friends to start praying for Jack. A cardiologist was on duty, and they did an emergency heart cath procedure. A major artery was severely blocked, and they put in a stent. There was some permanent damage to his heart, but one week after the procedure he was out on the golf course hitting a hole in one. My husband had quite a sense of humor, and he loved to tell people that my driving had caused his heart attack. Had he not been at the hospital when the heart attack occurred, the heart attack could very easily have been fatal. Again, I believed God's hand of mercy had moved on Jack's behalf, and my faith *and* Jack's faith continued to grow.

Jack had two other episodes with his heart. A few months later tests indicated that the stent might not be working, and he was hospitalized for another heart cath procedure. I prayed that the stent would work properly, and he would not have to have surgery. Immediately following the procedure, the nurse told him they had found nothing wrong, that the original test had evidently given a false positive result. Jack believed the nurse's report that the first test had given a wrong result, but I did not. I knew immediately that my God had again answered prayer and touched my husband. Again, my faith grew deeper and that cistern within me grew a little deeper.

The second incident occurred several years later. He was showing signs of another heart attack and was taken to the hospital by ambulance. My next door neighbor saw the ambulance and fire trucks at my home, and came over to ask how he could help. I asked him to drive me to the hospital, because it was evening and I am unable to drive after dark. I wanted to get to the hospital as quickly as possible to be with Jack. This particular neighbor had not lived next to us as long as our other neighbors had, but he and his wife were the exact support I needed at that particular time. They are strong Christians, and their family had personally experienced serious illness as their teenage daughter had gone through a lengthy battle with leukemia. They understood exactly what I was feeling. I mentioned to them that I did not even have the strength to pray, *and I was an intercessor.* I was emotionally very shaken at the thought of possibly losing my husband. They said they would pray for me, and they led us in prayer as they drove me to the hospital. They were my Aaron and Herr that evening. They stayed with me at the hospital until my family arrived. The doctor thought Jack was trying to develop a blood clot and that there was possibly a blockage. He spent the night in intensive care, and the next morning our doctor said he was transporting Jack later that day by ambulance to Kaiser's San Francisco hospital that specialized in heart problems. Before he left in the ambulance, I laid hands on his chest and prayed for the arteries to open and for the stent to work properly. My prayer partner Kim Staats said she had the following day off, so she offered to drive my granddaughter Terra and me to San Francisco. I grabbed my book "Sword of the Spirit" by Joy Lamb, and took it with me. It is a tool for intercessors that Kim and I have often used as we prayed for others. I told her that I was not going to let Jack go, and if he died I would be so emotionally upset that she was going to have to lead our prayer efforts. I told her we were going to pray him back to life if necessary. It was late when we arrived in San Francisco, so we spent the night in a hotel that the hospital had recommended. Early the next morning we went to the hospital and I met with Jack's nurse. They had completed some tests and had him scheduled for another heart cath. The nurse said there were indicators that open heart surgery might be needed, and doctors were available to do the surgery immediately if the heart cath confirmed their concerns. *Remember*, when the ambulance first took him to the hospital two days before, I was too shaken to pray. However, this time I felt such an overwhelming peace that he would be okay. that I was able to reach out and minister to someone else. Right after they took Jack into the operating room for the cath procedure, I noticed an elderly disabled woman in the waiting room all by herself. I could tell she was upset. I spoke to her, and learned that her husband had just had the same procedure as Jack, but he was not doing well. He was not stabilized enough for her to see him. They were on vacation in the mountains when the emergency occurred, and he had to be transported to San Francisco by ambulance. They did not have any family or friends in San Francisco to help them. She was all alone and frightened. I asked her if she would like Kim and me to pray with her, and she was very appreciative. We prayed with her and asked specifically for her husband's condition to be stabilized. Almost immediately after we finished praying, a nurse came and told her that her husband was now stabilized and she could see him. At the same time, Jack's nurse came into the waiting room and told me they could find absolutely nothing wrong with him. Jack was not to be released until the next day, but Kim had to return home that night. Jack had been transported to the hospital by ambulance quickly, so he didn't have any of his clothes with him. Kim, Terra, and I went shopping to buy something for him to wear home the next day when they released him. Terra and I were to stay the additional night, and my brother-in-law was going to drive to the city to help me take Jack home. Kim had to return that evening, as she was scheduled to work the next day. After we shopped, the Lord really impressed upon her that she was to be back at the hotel by 8:00 p.m. She had her hand on the door knob of our hotel room, ready to leave for home at exactly 8:00 p.m., when the Holy Spirit came over her. The three of us ended up in deep intercession for the City of San Francisco for the next three hours. We had no doubt in our minds that the San Francisco trip that had began as an 'emergency' situation for my husband had turned into a divine appointment for us. We had interceded for the City of San Francisco, ministered to a woman in need, and again witnessed God's answer to prayer for my husband's healing. Yes, my faith received a real booster shot on that trip, and Jack's faith also increased.

Some time later, Jack started having a lot of stomach problems. We had been told previously that he had a hernia caused from several surgeries associated with his gall bladder surgery. The stomach problems continued for quite some time, and the pain escalated. You could visibly see a large bump in his stomach. Our doctor ordered a CAT scan, and on the 4th of July, the doctor called us in the midst of our family Independence Day celebration to give us the results of the scan. When you receive a call from your doctor on a holiday, you know the news is not good. We were told that there appeared to be a lymphoma type mass in his abdomen, and the doctor was scheduling him to see a surgeon for a biopsy. Before the biopsy could be arranged, Jack woke up one morning with a mass on his neck that was over an inch long. We immediately called the doctor, and he was referred to another specialist. A biopsy on the neck is not as complex as one of the stomach, so that was done. We were told that he did have lymphoma and it was at stage 4. He was hospitalized so chemotherapy could start immediately. The mass on his neck literally dissolved as quickly as it had originally appeared. Again, my faith soared and I was so sure that God was again going to heal my husband. Again, that cistern within me grew larger. He went through a series of chemotherapy treatments. We were told that the lymphoma was in remission, and we were encouraged and hopeful that he had been healed. However, a few months later the oncologist told us the lymphoma had returned. The Lord really started dealing with me, asking me as I prayed if I was willing to give him my first love. He asked me if I trusted him. The very next day I received a devotional in my email about the story of Abraham and how the Lord had asked him to sacrifice his son Isaac. I was obedient, and told the Lord I trusted him and would surrender my will to his. I hoped God would spare Jack as he did Isaac, but I also knew this might not happen. My constant prayer for Jack was "May your kingdom come and your will be done in Jack's life. I surrender my will to yours, Lord, but the desire of my heart is that he be healed." When friends offered to pray for Jack, I asked them to pray for God's will to be done. Jack again went through a series of chemo treatments, and radiation treatments were also ordered. In January of 2009 we were told he was in remission, and we were elated. We were able to celebrate our 50th wedding anniversary on Valentine's Day. We had always planned to have a large reception at our church on our 50th and possibly take a cruise. After all Jack had been through, we were just very thankful that Jack's life had been spared and a big celebration was no longer important to us. Our daughter hosted a small gathering at our home for just our family and a few close friends, which was exactly what we wanted and needed at that time. The remission was short lived, and the cancer quickly returned requiring additional radiation treatments.

Adonai

Adonai, Adonai,
Adonai, Adonai.
You are my Lord, Adonai.
I am your servant.
I surrender all to you.
There's a destiny
That you are calling me to.
I will heed your call.
I'll give you my all.

I worship you, my Adonai.
I worship you, Adonai.
Break me.
Mold me
Fill me.
Use me.
Make me all you want me to be.
My life is in your hands.
I surrender to your plans.
I give my life to you, my Adonai.
I give my life to you, Adonai.

Chapter 11 Reality Sets In

Ecclesiastes 3:1-2
There is a time for everything, and a season
for every activity under heaven: 2 a time to be
born and a time to die, a time to plant and a
time to uproot

In April of 2009, my husband's oncologist said the mass in Jack's neck was completely gone, but the mass in his stomach was not responding to treatment. The doctor ordered a biopsy of his stomach and scheduled another appointment with her for June 11. She said by then she would know if the stomach mass was the same type of cancer, and she would give him one more chemo treatment. She said she would give him the type of chemo that would not cause further damage to his heart. Waiting for the biopsy results was difficult, and it was getting more difficult for my husband to eat. I called the doctor's office on the 10th, and happened to get a charge nurse who had worked with Jack in the infusion center. I asked if the biopsy results were in, and at first she was not going to give me any information. However, after she reviewed his results she told me the biopsy was clear and there was no evidence of a malignancy. I immediately thought we might be dealing with the hernia that was originally diagnosed and asked if he could be referred to a surgeon to discuss possibly removing the mass. A couple of hours later, the oncologist called me personally and said she disagreed with the biopsy results. She said evidently a clean piece of tissue had been tested and went on to tell me that she had referred Jack's case to hospice. I knew hospice was only called in when the patient was nearing death. I asked her if we could expect him to have another three months, and she said no. She was very evasive, but I continued to press her for an answer. I was not expecting what she told me. She said he might have a couple of weeks to live, and possibly just a few days.

I was dealing with some mobility issues of my own at that time. When Jack first started his chemo, I was having so much trouble with arthritis that I could not walk from the parking lot to the infusion center without the use of a transport chair. Jack would push me in the wheelchair from the parking lot to the infusion center, and then I would help him while he was having the chemo treatment. I knew that with hospice much of the care is provided by the family, and I was worried that I might not be physically able to provide the care he needed. I went on a diet to lose some weight rapidly to help take some pressure off of my joints so I was able to stand and walk easier. I am an insulin dependant diabetic, and losing the weight so quickly resulted in my blood sugars dropping dangerously low a couple of times. I continued to pray, God strengthened me, and I was able to provide Jack with the care he needed in our home.

I believe Psalms 103:2-3 with all my heart. It says, "2 Praise the LORD, my soul, and forget not all his benefits—3 who forgives all your sins and heals all your diseases."

There is no doubt in my mind that my God heals all our diseases, but I also know this healing takes place in his time and where he chooses. Ecclesiastics 3 tells us *"There is a time for everything, and a season for every activity under heaven: A time to be born and a time to die."* God had proven his healing power so many times in Jack's life, but I was beginning to face the reality that this time he might complete Jack's healing in heaven. When hospice came into our home, Jack could not eat more than a few bites at a time and was virtually starving. The hospice nurse suggested a medication that was not a cure, but one that could possibly reduce the tumor enough where his quality of life would be better. It was like a miracle medication. He was immediately able to eat solid food again and regained his strength enough to enjoy some family outings and spend some quality time with the family saying his goodbyes in his own way.

As people came to encourage him, they left being the ones who were encouraged by him. He had become that spiritual head of our home. I remember the elders from our church coming to our home to pray for Jack, and when they finished Jack told them he wanted to pray for them. His courage was amazing. He told me he didn't want to die and leave the family, but he said he did not fear death. He had a strong faith in God and knew where he was going. On August 2, 2009 the hospice nurse told us the end was very close. I called our immediate family and a couple of his best friends. He told me he wanted to speak with each person privately. He had words of wisdom and encouragement for each of us as he met with each of us individually and said his private goodbyes. Even at the end as he knew death was near, he was concerned about me and my well being. I learned much later that he spoke to my brother-in-law and my sister, Jackie, and asked them if they would look after me. It did not dawn on me until a few months ago that the calendar date when he told me goodbye was the same calendar day that we had originally met. We first met August 2, 1958 and fifty one years later he told me goodbye on August 2, 2009.

On August 4, we knew he was in his final hours. He was very concerned about one of his dear friends and golf partners who claimed to be an agnostic. He had known this man since they were fifteen, and it was very important to Jack to have one last chance to witness to him. I called his friend and told him Jack would like to see him one more time. He was so weak by the time his friend arrived, that the only word he was able to speak was his friend's name. I asked him if he wanted me to speak for him, and he nodded yes. I explained to the friend that Jack was very worried about him. Because he did not have a personal relationship with Christ, I told him that Jack didn't want to break up their golf foursome in heaven.

As soon as his friend left, I told Jack I was going to be okay, and he didn't have to fight this anymore. He was too weak to speak, and he closed his eyes and did not open them again. We could not tell if he could hear us or not. I held his hand and started singing "Face To Face", a song I had written years before when I was having the flashbacks. Jack had always loved that song. A sweet smile appeared on his face, and I knew he could still hear what we said. Shortly after that he passed away. That same song was used at his memorial service.

Face To Face.
As I come into your presence,
My feet on Holy ground
The wonder of your glory all around.
I look into your face, Lord
Amazed at what I see
Your eyes of love looking just at me.
Face to face, face to face.
Here in the Holy of Holies
You greet me with your mercy and your grace.
Face to face, face to face.
O Lord, I feel your strength and power.
I know your love and grace
As I come into your presence
And I meet you face to face.

I know without a doubt, Lord
This is where I want to be
Forever in your presence
Your eyes of love on me
And my heart just overflows for
The mercy you have shown
And I humbly kneel
And bow before your throne.

Face to face, face to face.
Here in the Holy of Holies
You greet me with your mercy and your grace.
Face to face, face to face.
O Lord, I feel your strength and power.
I know your love and grace
As I come into your presence
And I meet you face to face.

To Everything There Is A Time
Ecclesiastes 3

To everything there is a time
To everything there is a season
A time to laugh, a time to cry
A time to live, a time to die
A time to mourn and a time to dance.
It is all for a good reason
Every time and every season.

You're the God of creation
All's according to your plan
You made everything beautiful in its' time
You set eternity in the hearts of men
Whatever is, has already been,
And what will be has been before
It is all for a good reason
Every time and every season.

To everything there is a time
To everything there is a season
A time to tear, a time to mend
A time for peace, a time to defend
A time to listen, and a time to speak
It is all for a good reason
Every time and every season

You made everything beautiful in its time
You set eternity in the hearts of men
Whatever is has already been
And what will be has been before
It is all for a good reason
Every time and every season

Chapter 12 A Time To Mourn

Psalms 62:6
"He alone is my rock and my salvation; he
is my fortress, I will not be shaken."

I Will Not Be Shaken

You are my rock
You are my salvation
My tower of strength
And I will not be shaken
I give my all to you
O Lord who sees me through
You are the Mighty King
Master of everything.
You are my rock
You are my salvation
My hiding place
And I will not be shaken.
Be shaken, be shaken____
I will not be shaken.

I was somewhat numb for days after Jack died. I had to look at the guest book to determine who attended his memorial service, because I could not remember. God literally carried me through that day.

Jack had been the 'glue' in our family, and everyone was dealing with his death in their own way. I had so much business to take care of and family issues to deal with that I was unable to grieve. I was a trained manager, so I did what I was used to doing. I kicked into auto pilot mode and dealt with each of the situations that were at hand. However, I did not deal with my grief. I didn't actually start to grieve until several months later. Losing someone you love dearly and have spent fifty years of your life with is not something you easily adjust to overnight. It has now been over two years since Jack's death, and I am still grieving his death. As I have prayed, the Lord has impressed upon me that it would take me three years to go through this stage in my life. This means I still have a year to go, and I am trying to take one day at a time. I would not have made it if it were not for my faith in God. Over the years, each time I saw God's hand move on my behalf and my prayers answered, my faith grew and my cistern deepened. The only thing that has sustained me as I have faced the challenges of this new chapter in my life is being able to draw strength from that supply of living water that is within me.

I joined a hospice support group, and this has been an invaluable tool for me. Even though the official group sessions only lasted eight weeks, we became such a close knit group of friends that fourteen months later we are still meeting for lunch weekly.

Anniversaries, birthdays, and other dates that have significant meaning to you are especially difficult times in the grieving process. Hospice encouraged us to journal. I did some journaling during the hospice classes, but I was not consistent about it. I remembered a few months ago how therapeutic writing music was when I was healing from the flashbacks. I don't know why I had not attempted to work through my grief by writing music. In fact, I had almost stopped writing music after Jack died. I decided to sit down and put my feelings into music. Within five minutes, I had a poem written. The next morning I read it and reminded myself that it was supposed to be a song. I sat down at my keyboard, and the music just began to flow. The song helped me address my memories and feelings. The song was very personal and spoke of our fifty years together. I am still unable to sing it without tears starting to flow. However, it did achieve an important purpose. I had reached a roadblock in my grieving process. Once again, pouring out my pain through my music had helped me achieve a breakthrough so I could continue to move through the grieving process towards healing. I know my God is in control. I will continue to tap into that living water he has placed within me. I know he is the master of the storm, and he will sustain me and lead me through this current storm in my life. .

Master of the Storm

Cold winds blow. The thunder sounds.
Lightning flashes across the sky.
These stormy days could really get me down,
But I know they will go by.

My God is still the master of the storm.
He can still the winds and calm the sea
He has not changed.
He's still the same.
Yesterday, today, and always
And he loves me so.
He is the master of the storm.

No matter what I may be going through
I know I am not alone.
He'll take my hand.
By me he'll stand
I'm with the master of the storm.

So cold winds blow
And thunder sound
You can't scare me anymore.
I serve the one who's in control
And I love him so.

My God is still the master of the storm.
He can still the winds and calm the sea
He has not changed.
He's still the same
He is the master of the storm.

Chapter 13 Adjusting to a New Season

Psalms 91:1-2 He who dwells in the shelter of the Most High will rest in the shadow of the Almighty. 2 I will say of the LORD, "He is my refuge and my fortress, my God, in whom I trust."

I lived with my parents until I married, so living alone is very new to me and it has been difficult adjusting to being alone. The loneliness at times is overwhelming. Even though I am very active, it is not unusual for me to not see anyone for a few days at a time. My husband did most of the driving after he retired, so I am gradually getting used to driving again. I have glaucoma and don't see well at night, so I do not drive at all when it is dark. This limits my activities considerably. I used to lead worship at Aglow and church activities, and Jack always carried my keyboard for me and helped me set it up. I physically can't lift it, so I now rarely accept invitations to play for programs. We used to entertain a lot in our home, and we always hosted the family Christmas Eve celebration. I stopped hosting this because it was too difficult for me physically to set up the extra tables and chairs without help.

I have battled shyness all of my life. I had no problem interacting with people when I was doing so "officially" such as at work or in the community as an elected official. However, interacting on the plain social level has always been more difficult for me. I thought I had made a lot of progress over the years, but after Jack's death I realized that I had always leaned on him in social situations. The progress I thought I had made wasn't really progress, but it was faith in my husband to support me in those social situations. He was very outgoing and friendly, and had no problem carrying on a conversation with anyone, even strangers. However, after my husband's death I found I was really struggling with the shyness all over again. I felt uncomfortable and out of place in social situations. I was even uncomfortable with some of the friends we had as a couple for years, and I no longer felt I really belonged without my husband.

Coping with loneliness has probably been the biggest challenge for me to get used to. Evenings especially are difficult since I don't drive at night and am confined to the house most evenings by myself. I have always found that volunteering to help others is a good way for me not to focus on my own problems. I have dealt with the grief by trying to stay very busy and productive. I taught a women's Bible study in my home for awhile, took on the chairmanship of the senior ministry at my church, and am organizing Aglow intercessors throughout our state to pray for our government. I have also agreed to be the president of a new Aglow chapter that has been established in my city.

I recognize that there is a major difference between being very busy for the purpose of remaining active and in actually trying to keep busy for the purpose of running away from my problem, the grief I am experiencing. I am trying to balance my schedule and continue to work through the grief while staying busy enough to keep me from dwelling on it. I know this is a temporary season I am experiencing, and God will lead me through it.

As I reflect on my own life, I know that God was able to take each trial that I have faced and bring good out of it by using it to make me stronger and teach me to stand in faith and persevere. When fear about my future tries to creep in, I remind myself of 2 Timothy 1:7 *"For God has not given us the spirit of fear; but of power, and of love, and of a sound mind."* I try not to lean on my own understanding of the situation at hand, but to trust God to help me make the right decisions. I trust my God completely. I remind myself that I am a living cistern, and I will continue to draw from that supply of living water that he has placed within me. He will continue to be my strength and my refuge. I know that he will use this trial just like all of the others I have faced in my life to strengthen me and refine me to so I may one day become that living cistern of gold that I long to be.

Lord, You Are My Song

Lord, you are my refuge
Lord, you are my song.
Lord, you give me strength each day,
The strength I need to carry on.
You're my fortress, my salvation
And I lift my voice in praise
From the North, the South,
The East, the West
I will praise your name.
Lord, you made the music
That burns in my heart so strong.
Lord, you are my refuge,
And Lord, You are my song.

So with every breath I take
I just want to make
A sacrifice of praise to you.
I bow down in adoration
To the God of all creation.
Your handiwork I see
In the beauty all about me.
Lord, you made the music
That burns in my heart so strong.
Lord, you are my refuge,
And Lord, you are my song.
You're my comfort in times of sorrow.
You are my hope, Lord.
You're my tomorrow
Lord, you made the music
That burns in my heart so strong
Lord, you are my refuge,
And Lord, you are my song.

You're My Everything O God

You're my everything, O God.
You're my everything, O God.
When I'm weak, Lord,
You are strong.
You give me strength
When my own strength is gone.
When everything about me
Just seems to go wrong,
I'll keep my eyes on you.
You always see me through.
You're my everything, O God.

Though through valleys I must go
You're there with me this I know
You're my everything, O God
Under Your mighty wings I'll stay.
You will guide me all the way.
You're my everything, O God.

You're my refuge,
You're my shield.
Unto your will, Lord,
I do yield.
You're my everything.
You're my everything.
You're my everything, O God.

Works Cited

http://www.bible.dictionary.org/cistern
Smith's Bible Dictionary

Would you like to see your manuscript become a book?

If you are interested in becoming a PublishAmerica author, please submit your manuscript for possible publication to us at:

acquisitions@publishamerica.com

You may also mail in your manuscript to:

**PublishAmerica
PO Box 151
Frederick, MD 21705**

www.publishamerica.com